Losers Dream On

PHOENIX POETS

MARK HALLIDAY

Losers Dream On

THE UNIVERSITY OF CHICAGO PRESS

Chicago & London

The University of Chicago Press, Chicago 60637
The University of Chicago Press, Ltd., London
© 2018 by The University of Chicago
Published 2018
Printed in the United States of America

27 26 25 24 23 22 21 20 19 18   1 2 3 4 5

ISBN-13: 978-0-226-53359-9 (paper)
ISBN-13: 978-0-226-53362-9 (e-book)
DOI: https://doi.org/10.7208/chicago/9780226533629.001.0001

Library of Congress Cataloging-in-Publication Data
Names: Halliday, Mark, 1949– author.
Title: Losers dream on / Mark Halliday.
Other titles: Phoenix poets.
Description: Chicago : The University of Chicago Press, 2017. | Series: Phoenix poets | Poems.
Identifiers: LCCN 2017018052| ISBN 9780226533599 (pbk. : alk. paper) | ISBN 9780226533629 (e-book)

Classification: LCC PS3558.A386 L67 2017 | DDC 811/.54—dc23 LC record available at https://lccn.loc.gov/2017018052

♾ This paper meets the requirements of ANSI/NISO Z39.48–1992 (Permanence of Paper).

Though infinite the damage we had wrought
To sit back folded in regret would make, we thought,
A mockery of everything we bravely sought
As if our truest beauties were not worth a fight—
Hence it felt right or as if right
To go on loving and desiring day and night.

Felicia Degringolade

And we say that repose has fled
For ever the course of the river of Time.
That cities will crowd to its edge
In a blacker, incessanter line;
That the din will be more on its banks,
Denser the trade on its stream,
Flatter the plain where it flows,
Fiercer the sun overhead.
That never will those on its breast
See an ennobling sight,
Drink of the feeling of quiet again.

But what was before us we know not,
And we know not what shall succeed.

Matthew Arnold

CONTENTS

Acknowledgments ix

*

Glen *3*
Bus Full of Dinosaurs *5*
Worthy *6*
First Wife *7*
Ernest and Lionel *8*
Hal Dead *9*
Chilled *12*
He Meant *13*
Index to *Hamaday: A Questionable Life* *16*
Thirteen Balloons *18*
66 Benevolent Street *19*

**

About Time *23*
Yearbook Photo *25*
Your New Assignment *26*
Moot *28*
Maria's Mexican Food *30*
Thin White Shirts *31*
Milano Adesso *33*
Bird's Shadow *34*
Poured *35*

***

Balancing Act *39*
Tossed Cup *40*
Not Exactly for Talia *41*

Freedom of Speech 42
Tradeoffs 43
Boomerang 45
Whizdizz 47
Shark Fate 48
Almost Dusk 49
After the Major Events 50

****

Angel at Wilkes 53
Their First Marriage 55
Sarah Sees Two Runners 57
A Gender Theory 59
The Quilmias 60
Your Paltry Conquests 62
Shadblow 63
Been There 64
Our Love Problem 65
Midnight, the Stars and You 66

*****

You Lament 69
Not Nothing 70
Whisk Broom 73
Rolf Smedvig in Particular 74
But Also 75
My Other Apartment 77
Plot Twist 79
No Vacation for Maigret 80
Meaning 82

ACKNOWLEDGMENTS

Some of these poems have appeared in journals:

The Cincinnati Review: "Milano Adesso" and "Our Love Problem"
The Cortland Review (online): "Glen"
Ecotone: "Bus Full of Dinosaurs"
The Florida Review: "First Wife"
The Gettysburg Review: "Not Exactly for Talia"
The Hopkins Review: "Your New Assignment"
The North: "Midnight, the Stars and You"
Ploughshares: "A Gender Theory" and "No Vacation for Maigret"
Virginia Quarterly Review: "About Time"

"Been There" (as "Impelled to Hark") appeared in *The Heart's Many Doors*, edited by Richard Jackson (San Antonio: Wings Press, 2017)

GLEN

Back and back over the meadows and through the groves
and back and beyond the broken speckle-gray boulders
there is a shady road that curves downward into a glen.
Along down the shady road of powdery dust I go.
Till the glen is near—

If I tell you that a typed copy of "Waving Adieu, Adieu, Adieu"
was taped to the kitchen wall of my humble apartment in 1988
you don't start to cry. You just look intelligent
with a polite smile, waiting for a metaphor.

Allusion is an admission of insufficient present power;
a wish to borrow power from an old source.

Nick my baby blond boy crawled to the doorway
and pulled himself up by gripping the doorframe
and demanded to be part of the conversation in the kitchen.
On the wall above him was the poem by Stevens.

Back and back—till the glen is near—
while all the shady branches along the road already
have disappeared behind you . . .

Allusion is an admission that the painful recognitions of loss
have been lived through before. It means we have old comrades
in the never-completed negotiation.

When I jotted this in a notebook Nick was in college
pondering what can be represented; he became
an artist fascinated by layers and time's erosions.

Someone could paint a shady dusty road making you feel
how the glen with its divertimenti of thrush and wren
is leaving already even as you step down farther into its shade.
You could appreciate this painting and put on your wall
a photo of it and then twenty-plus years later
you might need to tell someone how it was there
twenty-plus years back and back. To say "We knew, we did know,
we weren't idiots! We knew everything was departing."

That small yellow kitchen; Nick, my golden boy,
standing up all by himself.

BUS FULL OF DINOSAURS

We loved to turn the page and see the bus full of dinosaurs
and say, "*This* is not the bus to the park!
"*This* is the bus to the Natural History Museum!"
Hilarious, over and over
twenty-plus years ago when my son was little.

Because its inviting of sympathy is coercive
little is one of the words you should probably dodge in a poem
along with *nice, delicious, excellent, gorgeous, sublime* . . .

How many more such nice memories can bubble into consciousness
before the sublimity factory ceases production?
Just say it's excellent that they flare up now and again
during our coercive mass transit to extinction,
gorgeous for a second in the dark.
This is not the bus to the park.

WORTHY

The three-year-old boy on his dad's shoulders at the airport
would be thrilled to see a plane take off—
the dad keeps trotting from one giant lounge window to another
but they keep arriving a few seconds too late,
the plane is already gone—no, to be fair

a few times they do see a plane rush along the runway
in a purity of certainty and confidence
until it goes beyond their angle of vision—
and once maybe they do see the moment of liftoff!

Anyway the boy forgives his dad for being slow—
the boy can tell the dad is trying, and the rushing is
exciting in itself—and the dad is happy because he knows
he is trying: he feels that being a good dad is worthy
in a sturdy kind of way, it's a kind of worthiness

that does not turn out to be delusory or hollow
which is why he will need to remember all this
twenty-three years later in an airport with his rollerbag
and secret doubt and nothing on his shoulders.

FIRST WIFE

Each of us carries secret scars in spirit always ready
to be wakened into wounds, ready as if waiting
as if to be wakened into wounds is a debt forever unpaid;
a song suddenly brings the invoice again
and finds the screen door forever unlatched—

as when I hear "Save the Last Dance for Me"
and think immediately of Annie
and how I always said I would.

ERNEST AND LIONEL

On this cardboard coffee cup from Ernest Klein Market
there is a design with little gold stars bedecking a dark blue ribbon.
This is an example of the splendor of human contriving.
My father, who will be dead within two months, is unspeakably tired
yet glad to be conscious in the realm of human contriving
where the dark blue ribbon bears these tiny gold stars.
Kids love star shapes, they know the shape implies sublimity.
We find sublimity in the world (stars in the sky) and we make
sublimity for the world (the design on a coffee cup). I am thinking
these calm thoughts
as my father breathes studiously in his last June. I want

to live and live and live—despite whatever stupidities
and humiliations—and my father still wants this too even if
diminishingly. He has us listen to Lionel Hampton playing
"China Stomp" in 1937, and sixty-six years later we feel
sort of secretly gaga at the sublimity pouring through this
small apartment, "China Stomp" lives insouciantly forever and we
who are not dead listen.

HAL DEAD

There far amid the towers of Gotham sits old Hal
upon the blue couch slumped, unseeing the *Times*.
Go call his sons the careful Kim and anxious Mark
Call them hither to summon the men who dispose

and to speak with the neighbors and the superintendent
and to carry the cat by cab to its final place
for there are duties and decisions to be made
in the silent apartment amid the towers

The clouds bloom darkly silent over the city
The traffic honks and jerks forward without meaning
Huge plastic bags of day-old loaves lie
in the gutter outside Au Bon Pain on 55th

and so the sons must come and speak with the disposers
for Hal is dead. For Hal is dead
and so through the ways of Gotham past Godondra
unto the third-floor haunted cave they come

as Odin mounts his horse Sleipner and rides away
to Lidskialf and sits there invisible upon his throne
and Skulda and Hoder and Frea do their cloudy tasks
along the cobbled avenues of shadowed Asgard

The LPs and CDs go into boxes, Maria Muldaur
and all the torch singers and all the big band jazz and swing
and the books on Jefferson and Madison and liberty
go into boxes, into heavy boxes taped and double-taped

9

the boxes heavy and yet the loads feel stupidly light
on the curving stairs down and down to the waiting cars
for things cannot be left untouched in the haunted cave
when Odin has galloped away into the secret clouds.

O'er the bridge Bifrost, where Heimdall watches
and through the glen where Fensaler stands
and past the house of Frea and past Ernest Klein Grocery
and through the wood of Jarnvid where the trees are iron

ride the sons of Hal with helplessly creaking boxes
past Muspel's fires and Midgard fort and stony Godondra towers
and past the harbor where Regner's ship floats on dark current
where Liberty raises her torch forever

for Madison and Jefferson and ever for Hal
who had strong shoulders and strong views
and believed that we are all impassioned clay
and in long Gotham evenings spoke gently to his cat Cleo

but lastly rode alone alone alone unto the plain of Niflheim
where dwell the dead, and thence to the darkest lake
unseen by Heimdall or by Frea and by his sons unseen,
the lake of Breidablik from which no bubble rises—

Yet even in the abode of death, O Hal, hail!
Even in the shadows out at the secret end of flinty Asgard
where no honking of Gotham's taxis can be heard!
Tonight there is hot fondue at La Bonne Soupe on 55th

and the couples chuckle after Broadway shows
and Kim and Mark must also laugh a little, they must
while Odin mounted on Sleipner gallops away
past Chrysler tower and down and down through stony Asgard

away unto his secret silent fate as nights do pass
and days must pass which is all the nights and days can do—
the hoofs of massive Sleipner ring upon the distant stones
while Gotham's cooks serve up new messes of

the boar Serimner's blooded flesh for all the living,
and Frea dines and Heimdall dines, and scheming Lok,
Skulda dines and Hoder, and Kim and Mark cannot choose
not to dine upon the roasted flesh of Serimner.

Oh sons of Hal why tarriest thou in the gulph of inner gloom?
Let the Valkyries fill thy goblets with mead!
For we are Bronx and Brooklyn diners all
no matter how we honk or mourn or fret

so seek therefore the golden dice with which you play'd of yore;
enforc'd is Odin's absence from the fields of war and broils
and nights and days can only be this passing though Hal is dead
and you must ride away through Jarnvid where the trees are iron.

CHILLED

Quite adroitly for so many years
he has avoided being an old man

yet now he is somehow a very old man
and he gets sudden chills
when everyone else feels the temperature is pleasant.
Ten minutes ago it happened
on the way back to his son's house or his daughter's house—

the shivering came over him, he tried furiously to conceal it
rigidly tensing his skinny old muscles
but then when the others lingered outside to chat with a neighbor
he panicked and began to moan and gasp in outrage
knowing how exactly this made him like a baby.
His son or daughter led him into the warm house
where he sits now with a blanket over his knees—

staring at the floor, staring into the heart of injustice,
no longer shivering but still
locked in silent black fury against
the cheerful stupid chatty tribe of the not old.
The year is 2037. His name is Mark.

HE MEANT

He meant not to vanish.
He meant to make a shape.
To appreciate. To mean.
Not forever to be a teen!

———

He worked on his line breaks as a means toward im-
mortality

———

Rain down on the dogs of time.
In the confusion we crossed the street.

———

Damn long time ago that he and his friend Eric tried
to co-author a thing that started "In the confusion
we crossed the street"—more than forty years ago
and their big feeling was bafflement and now
his big feeling is still bafflement with some wrinkles.
Someone should love him for his bafflement.

———

Dozens of smart sharp rhythmic women are moving
through the Detroit airport
what to do oh god

———

Maggie P. is gone.
Lisa W. is gone.
Jan where are you?
In her room on the third floor
Julie kept humming to herself.
Heavy dark ledgers of the ungiven and unshared.

———

He stared into space at odd moments and became
briefly less trivial; with what useful result?

———

Passed bumbling through this world.
Ping-pong ball of self

———

There is some basic firm evidence of identity:
At least the old tweed jacket from Uncle Lew
the Coffee Kids cap
the AS 220 t-shirt
At least the bold firm marginal notes in these paperbacks
and those paperbacks
At least the ability to imitate Alex Chilton doing "The Letter"
At least the being a sweet daddy for the little girl—
"Is Spot in the box? No, it's some penguins!
Where is Spot? Let's turn the page."

———

He meant and the years scrummed and bashed and swooshed
and he sent some pretty clever emails remarking on this

———

When he shifted his load on Hope Street
the book that tumbled out of his bag of laundry was
Death and Modern Man by Jacques Choron.
Jessica said, "You crazy monkey,
six dollars for death would be bad enough,
must we have modern man as well?"
He said, "I want to be a thinker."
"Think box of Fab," she said.

———

Like a ping-pong ball with a PhD
these fragments have I yah yah yah

———

He meant to try to learn to show energetic compassion
for other humans—insofar as it is learnable

———

That earthquake in Haiti happened in January 2010 killing
200,000 if that is conceivable and I cared consciously for five days
even maybe eight days and sent fifty dollars

———

By the time I was in that hospital cafeteria in 1974
staring at a stupid dank hamburger
it was already too late to make Bev happier
by joking in French or singing "Be Back Soon"
or another song I can't think of and can't ask her.

INDEX TO *HAMADAY: A QUESTIONABLE LIFE*

Addicted to salted cashews,   64

Apologizes to two women in past,   55

Baffled by human acquiescence in gush of time,   49

Complacently accepts middle-class white male privilege,   56

Considerably less funny than thinks,   66

Doubts greatness of Philip Roth,   49

Dozes off over important books,   38, 39, 40, 41, 42, 43, etc.

Eats more than friends deem possible,   19, 20, 22, 24, 26, 28, 31ff

Feels "smaller than his life,"   57, 62

Forgets smart things said in restaurants,   28, 33, 39, 47, 60

Forgets that everyone else's heart is beating,   38, 48, 58

Honors Paul Violi via less funny imitation,   see Index

Hopes candor can substitute for lapidary brocade,   38

Hopes mild flickering wit better than no wit,   67

Jilted by series of women insensitive to poetic virility,   23, 24, 26, 27 ff.

Keeps daily diary because is center of world,   41

Loses track of criteria for good poems,   45, 55, 67

Means more than can quite express,   *passim*

Melon balls, metaphorical references to,   33, 44

More talented than enemies, by long shot,   48

More talented than friends, why not admit,   58

Mutters to self, unaware of being observed,   59–65

Ogles young women in airports,   45–66

Opposes own sexist tendencies,   24, 47, 56

Plans day around caffeine,   43, 45, 46, 48, 50, 52, etc.

Rejects "reference," "impact," and "grow" as transitive verbs,   54

Resents smart males in their thirties and forties,   57–65

Salves conscience by sending small contributions to

Amnesty International, Planned Parenthood, Doctors Without Borders
     and ACLU,   32, 40, 50, 61
Sings like George Thorogood while alone in car,   62
Still trying to impress women unimpressed forty years earlier,   61
Suddenly sees self as tiny fleck of ego amid billions of such,   70
Surprisingly clever after two gin and tonics,   56
Testosterone in odd relation to existential bafflement,   51, 55, 60
Time, mystery of, unable to stop exclaiming about,   39, 49, 59
Undeserving of luck but very glad to have it,   68
Wishes had been kinder on certain occasions,   71

THIRTEEN BALLOONS

Jill's dad turns eighty-seven today.
Jill strings up thirteen balloons above the space
between kitchen and dinner table and all day
they jostle gently in the invisible currents of time.
I mean air. Yellow, blue, red, plus a random black one
not used last Halloween. Why thirteen balloons,
no special reason, it just happened that way.
Gently they jostle above us through the hours
while Jill bakes the cake and arranges on the frosting
an 8 and a 7 with candy stars.
Someone lets the cat in from outside,
our cat Abbie, queen of alert self-interest.
She glances up at the strangely subtly moving balloons
and decides: nothing to worry about there.

66 BENEVOLENT STREET

Calliope fly with me now to 66 Benevolent Street
where on the sloping blue floor of the past
Arlo Guthrie sings "My Creole Belle" over and over
and young Mark frowns at the dreariness of Saul Bellow
as Jessica mutters conjugations of Spanish verbs.

Calliope lend me thy silver harp to play the scene
where Paul Hertz answers the phone by saying "Telephone"
and two guys named John ate our big box of River Rice
so Jessica calls them the river rats
and she cleans the tiny kitchen because we are nearly adults
and after passion she always says she craves lime juice

O Calliope protect and enshrine this tiny chalice
as if not infinitesimal, this cup of dreamt memory
in which the bumpy blue floor is thrillingly chilly
under bare feet rushing toward the narrow bed

and in the dining room one night
either Joel or Jim hides a plastic pistol under Mark's spaghetti
as if he were a prisoner as if youth were not a glorious haven
and on the bathroom wall is taped a long passage from "Comus"
in which desire and vanity temptingly intertwine

at 66 Benevolent Street where Jessica requires young Mark
to sprinkle foot powder in his egregious sneakers
O Calliope do not omit the notion of Poetry burbling there, Poetry
whereby the detritus becomes constellated forever
burbling there at 66 Benevolent where one day Mark wrote

"Monday's Cello" having caught on to the mentholated style
that seemed to promise Fame ah this was silly
but supremely forgiven by thee, kind Calliope,
forgiven and embraced! Or so I require to believe.
And let it circle back, good goddess, that song I remember well,
and let it for aye be cupped in meaning, "My Creole Belle."

ABOUT TIME

About time I will in 2023 say things inadequate
under a compulsion to face my enemy,
to look my destroyer in the eye—time
which has no eye, no face
and will evade whatever I say by the sly simple strategy of
never stopping. I knew this in 1992
and tried to say it! In my kitchen I felt there was
a great ship plowing toward the horizon
and me swimming in its salty wake unrescued.
The big green refrigerator hummed
awfully loudly if you paused to notice
and the maple leaves out there past my unstable balcony
shifted gently in the rainy breeze
like the beginnings of ideas about time that never
got anywhere. The actual present that day was
as it is now a whirldazz dazzwhirl of signals
not quite meshed, even in a peaceful kitchen.
It is
        the naked skinless edge of This Day
which is a dubious overproduced emergency
requiring hundreds of gearings of courage and caution
just to keep the favorite organism oneself operative
in the casually harmful flux. Today though
is oddly
          just the tense palpable portion of
This Week
              which is really only the most noisy and distracting
scout or tentacle or probe or exploratory mission sent from
These Last Two Months

which are really
the future, the immediate future, the terrain of
an as yet unmanaged disorderly over-budget pilot version
of what you expected to have to struggle with
plus five odd bits of bad luck and one of good;
thus meanwhile
the real present, the *real* present
is Two Months Ago where you reached
a clarity you could live in, some provisional understanding
of what your life had come to
and how you'd get ready to ride on the rest,
ready for your life you poor brave child
and never fall behind.

YEARBOOK PHOTO

We the editors of this year's Yearbook regret to inform you
that due to certain errors in our production process
the caption under your photo, instead of reading
Most Likely to Achieve Something Original
reads *Most Likely to Accumulate Big Boxes of Unpublished Manuscripts*
Full of Banal Imaginary Sexual Adventure.
Also, in some copies of the Yearbook
the photo that accompanies your name is for some reason
not of you wearing your dark blue silk tie
but of a self-grooming baboon.
Production of this year's Yearbook involved new technologies
which introduced errata beyond our conscious control.
We hope the Yearbook will be useful to you
despite these acknowledged flaws
and will help you remember your present identity
when you have, hypothetically, moved on to other stages of life.
At this time, also, we would like to remind you
that in sixty years or less
this new Yearbook will be a wad of ash at the bottom of an incinerator
or else an ancient text as strangely fictive and absurdly remote
as *Beowulf* seems to your most unimaginative classmates.
Nevertheless, we recognize that you probably will be perturbed
by the errors affecting your Yearbook profile
and in that sense they are regrettable.

YOUR NEW ASSIGNMENT

Not to exaggerate anything and I admit I've had too much sugar today
and my head aches a little but I kind of want to complain
to Bethany Hubbard, Madison Pirrone, Will Studer, Emma Swintek,
Danielle Bishop, Bryannah Dailey, Patrick Fisher, and Christopher Flake

because I happened to pull out the file on English 250 in Fall 2011
and I see that you never came and picked up your final papers
on *Hamlet* and *The House of Mirth* but I suspect that now,
more than five years later, you have begun to sense that life

washes away! Life washes away from us at all ages
and we need to *grip* it to the extent that we can grip it—
but you just abandoned your final papers, a few of them quite good,
others riddled with weaknesses, upon which in all cases I wrote

detailed thoughtful comments in the margins—this took me hours,
hours! Hours of my one life. I was trying to *help* you—
help you care about poor brilliant Hamlet who fears that life
is absurdly pointless—remember the graveyard scene?

You may not recall but we had a damned good discussion of it.
And about brave unwise Lily Bart who keeps imagining
mere beauty and charm can triumph over time....
Oh, don't say you'll come and get your final papers now, don't even pretend,

it's too late! I just chucked them in the recycling bin!
Your assignment now is for you to reflect on

what your abandoned papers imply about your priorities
and about our lives, our fate, and if you find you have something to say

send me 200 words on this, double-spaced, before the Christmas break.

MOOT

Seen from up here
the students crisscrossing the brick patio
with their plastic cups and their clunky backpacks
and their thumbs texting "blew the quiz" or "buy beer"
are interchangeable bits of humanity

No they are not interchangeable
each is a unique complex of feeling and perception
and thought and memory and arguably soul

Sorry no they are mere specks of animate flesh
seen from this bench on the hill
the bitsy variations don't matter

Yes they do matter
Why do they matter
The question "Why do they matter" is moot
Why is it moot
That question is also moot
Why moot

Because of the edge in your voice when you ask the question
because you only pretend it is a cool objective question
whereas an answer to the question is hidden in your voice
because of how you want me to hear you asking the question
as we sit side by side watching the students down there
wending their ways through the throng each with intentions
frustrated only a little or perhaps severely frustrated

but still getting coffee and comparing notes
because they can't help being interested in their lives

while you want me to notice that you are the one asking
the bravely cold questions here today
on this bench on the yellow-grass hill
where you and not someone else are the one caring to ask

while I can feel how you just ten inches away
already understand how moot are your questions here today.

MARIA'S MEXICAN FOOD

At 8 p.m. on a Monday night in San Diego
Maria's Mexican Food is already closing and I am the only customer
and they want me to leave soon but I will calmly finish
my enchiladas rojas, I don't need to feel tense or silly,
why should I? Just because I'm alone and am trying to substitute
gustatory pleasure for purposeful action toward a worthwhile
moral objective or spiritual search? Surely purposefulness and searching
can't be unmistakably visible all day every day. Surely
the best workers in Doctors Without Borders or Amnesty International
occasionally sit alone with average enchiladas!
It occurs to me now that in Philadelphia it is 11 p.m.
and I know there's a guy in a Mexican restaurant near the Delaware River
in the same situation, because I was exactly there in 1993,
the waitress is actually beginning to mop the floor—

Listen my brother! Do not quail!
You are within your rights and you are not a pathetic cipher.
Go ahead and fork up those last bits of salsa and rice.
I see you there, O my brother, you are not alone
in this darkening vale of closing restaurants;
do not quail in the vale
for I in San Diego am with you in Philadelphia
defiant of space, defiant of our ostensibly drastic isolation!
Courage, far brother there near the chilly Delaware:
stand tall and leave a decent tip and slowly stroll forth.

THIN WHITE SHIRTS

My father said some smart things when he was very old
but also when he was in his fifties; if there is a wisdom of age
the wisdom is mainly not new in content,
in declarable themes; we understood *Hamlet*
and even *Lear* in the way of declarable meanings
when we were twenty; and Donovan Leitch sang
"The Ballad of Geraldine" so poignantly
when he was nineteen: awareness of human pathos
was there in his voice—and I did hear that
in 1967 when I was eighteen—but

there is still a wisdom of age that will be perceptible
in you—eventually—
reading and listening again—again—with your history
of failures and blindnesses in the myriad human moments

giving a weight to certain perceptions not a heavy
weight of knowledge but a light accumulation
like dry snow on a pearl-gray morning—

there was a tender tone in which my father read aloud
When lofty trees I see barren of leaves,
Which erst from heat did canopy the herd—a tone
not heavy; instead an accumulated lightness

like a thousand white shirts
white shirts terribly thin and light
having been so many times worn and washed and worn

a thousand white shirts heaping up and the next one always
coming silent to rest on the top—

not what you "know" about our weakness and possible goodness
our failing our dying
but the quiet long layeredness with which you know it

MILANO ADESSO

They are speaking rapidly in Milan right now unacceptably
far from me at tables in sunlight, their sunglasses poised adeptly
upon their dark hair, their hands inflecting thoughts,
they understand themselves to be splendidly alive *adesso*
and to waste it would be a provincial sort of stupidity
somehow not unrelated to American crudity
so they laugh bright-briefly and pivot into
the next current in their silver stream of Milanese
in which they take for granted three or seven insights
cultural, political, postindustrial millennial digital
toward which I will stumble three or five years hence if
even then. Light breeze flicks the piazza
causing quick adjustments of handsome intelligent hair
in Milan right now as the conversation pivots like a skier
S-curving through implications of non-stupid passion
(with irony incorporated) sexual certainly though
inseparable from books and fifty websites I will
never visit.
         Milan, Milano,
Milano *adesso si* far far aye aye flow on great Po
great Danube mighty Rhine aye ripple on old Seine

in a Kansas of muddled passive co-optedness though I be
while brightness streams on elsewhere mythically
we shall all quicksoon enough find the sea!

BIRD'S SHADOW

The unavailability of a culmination
is a bird's shadow that passes over you
twice a week or is it twice a day—

there won't be a shapely fulfilled shape—
there will only be the box heaped with provisional
efforts some detectably defter or heavier than others but
all provisional until
an arbitrary ending suddenly—

I'm looking at my old correspondence with a friend who will
probably not live much longer
there's no culmination there's no rounding it all off there's
no beautiful farewell thick with violins

—there's only the heap of memos palimpsested in the years

as when on a cold street in Denver he said
apropos of I forget what
that although Shelley was such a haplessly harmful man
Shelley's letters are oddly moving
because of his inability to stop aspiring
amid fiascos and deflections
for some honorable culmination.

POURED

What if it is all just given
and given and given and given
(not by a giver but by the fierce bubbling persistence of DNA)
and given and given for no purpose given
poured into your hands poured unearned
through your hands flooded through you

until you can't cope with the abundance
and your little network of receptors and transformers deteriorates
amid the blazing flood of the given
till you murmur your last request for H_2O
and your hand falls on the bedsheet
and you are gone into compost with no accounting
with no ledger with no invoice for ridiculously huge debt
no inventory of your hapless bitsy gestures toward payment
(except family and friends who occasionally recall you did X or Y)

—what if all that?

Indeed what. By the by, did you write some odd interesting thing
in your small notebook in 1983? Show me.

BALANCING ACT

Over on that side,
grotesque injustices and monstrous misfortunes
and chaos of incomprehensible social dynamics

and on this side,
little Marky with his muffin.

TOSSED CUP

We participate in systems.
Individually we have not exactly chosen them
though we do acquiesce in them.

Do you suppose there is an airport custodian who feels loathing
for travelers who toss all sorts of messy trash into trash receptacles
with no worry about waste? How could there not be?
A custodian possibly named Consuela or Takrim.

At airports I always want coffee
but I never drink the whole cup—it's always too much;
but if I say I want the cup half full the barista thinks
I'm a little odd and even slightly annoying—
and may suspect that I want to pay half price.

Suddenly my plane is boarding
and I have four ounces of unwanted coffee!
Do I run to the Men's Room?
No—I dump the cup in the trash.

Months go by, years go by, a hundred thousand planes take off
and Takrim or Consuela is still dealing with airport trash—
hot coffee leaks through holes in the trash bags
and Consuela feels dreary loathing or Takrim feels bitter loathing
while I fly away jotting down interesting thoughts.

NOT EXACTLY FOR TALIA

The supermarket cashier working Saturday night
rang up my yogurts and Milano cookies.
Her name plate said *Talia*, I think.
Just as she was about to give me my change
and I was saying "Thanks a lot"
a young grocery clerk passed behind her and murmured some remark
and moved rapidly away so Talia said loudly "*Shut up!*"
in the tone that nowadays means "Your remark is silly
and even a little irritating but more enjoyable than irritating
but don't think you can dominate me by surprising me"—

and then suddenly she feared that I,
the balding white customer, might imagine she had said it to me
whereupon we shared a half second of humanly real eye contact

and then she gave me an actual warm smile with my change
and I gave her back an actual warm smile to show
I understood everything she could hope I would understand
and she said "Have a good one" meaning a good evening
as if she meant it more than she could usually mean it

so then I walked out with my bag of cookies and yogurts
to have a good benevolent evening while Talia stayed
to work the register at Acme on Saturday night.

Now, what is that panting squeaking sound?
It is the sound of a dozen heroically moral theorists of race and class
lurching straining to be the first
to demolish my liberal humanist complacency before I reach my car.

FREEDOM OF SPEECH

February 11, 2017

While we stood with candles in the chilly evening
two hundred yards from the White House
listening to speakers exhorting us to resist tyranny,
to fight hate with love,
five hundred of us cheering on cue,
most of us writers doing this "act of resistance"
on the last night of our vastly un-urgent writers' conference,
Vladimir Kara-Murza lay barely out of a coma in Moscow
with "heavy metals" in his blood,
Vladimir Kara-Murza, victim (for the second time)
of a "mystery toxin" more decisive than
the nice little shot of warmth we felt as we cheered with candles
and we chanted that we want truth *now* and poetry *now*.

...But ironic juxtaposition is easy.
You live in the life you have
and you try to be awake.

TRADEOFFS

The thing these liberals never understand
is that politics is always tradeoffs—
you can't get *everything* you want so you make choices.
For instance, this whole question about climate change
and how it comes from greenhouse gases from burning fossil fuels–
I don't say they're wrong about this.
I was skeptical fifteen years ago, but apparently
there's a lot of scientific evidence, all right, so,
yes, in an ideal world we would shift over
to things like solar and wind power (but
China and India and Russia and Brazil and Mexico,
by the way, would have to do the same)—but here's the thing:
there would be a tradeoff. For instance,

if I started really pushing for this there would definitely be
a tradeoff in concrete terms. For instance,
I come up for re-election in three years.
If I were to get all gung ho about cutting carbon emissions
I would have some major enemies lining up to knock me down.
Big oil, big coal, plus all their allies, those guys can hit and hit hard.
They can outspend any environmental types five to one.
Do I want to lose and be just some ex-senator
who serves on some board of trustees? Whereas,
if I get re-elected, I am in a position to be seriously helpful
to some really good people—not just a few dozen,
I'm talking *hundreds* of good people. I can be seriously instrumental
in developing the careers of truly almost a thousand people
who in one way or another count on me to advance certain agendas
and certain projects that unquestionably benefit some very good people.

Look at these photos on my phone—those are my nephews—
and those are my daughters with their kids—and this is my executive secretary
with her family—her brother managed my campaign upstate—
these are all wonderful people. They count on me.
And they have people who count on them. Wider and wider circles,
so to speak. So when I look at any big policy consideration,
I have to think in terms of what is the real tradeoff. In this case,
on the one hand, yes, in fifty years apparently all the coastal cities will be
totally flooded, and thousands of animal species will go extinct,
and the oceans will be fouled and seafood will practically not exist,
yadda yadda, and various other big effects of global warming.
On the other hand, I can quite directly and positively improve the lives
of *hundreds* of unquestionably good people throughout the next
two decades at least! So there are things to consider on both sides
and it behooves me to weigh the options very carefully.

BOOMERANG

Sure, you can use the word "grandchildren" as a sort of political weapon,
but seriously … Can we be frank? My picture of the big future of society
is almost as dire as yours. Myself, I have one daughter
and I will strongly advise her to only have one kid
and I plan to make damn sure there's a *ton* of money in the bank
for that kid's future—so that he or she will be able to buy
the technology and status and protection that will make life still livable
in, you know, the 2030s and 2040s etc. Because

naturally I am going to love that one kid—my grandchild. But
what I'm saying—basically what I'm saying is this:
setting aside how you might feel about your *own* cute little grandchild,
and looking instead at the broader picture:

why does it matter if the world is going to hell?

People keep moaning about global warming, air pollution, water pollution,
yadda yadda—hey, I know those things are real, I'm not an idiot!
But here's the point: why does it *matter*
if human life turns all grim and bitter in, like, fifty years?
People act like "Oh, that's so tragic!" But if you think about it
who cares if a thousand coastal cities go underwater
and thirty million people die in floods and landslides and typhoons,
whatever—so what? Sixty million, so what?
Plus two billion others starving in blistering hot deserts?
Those poor losers will be just little human beings, nothing more.
They sure as hell won't be saints! They will be unlucky examples
of the species that fucked everything up. Why let your heart bleed
for those losers? Wrong place, wrong time, folks!

Look at it objectively: the whole human trip has been an experiment
in cleverness without wisdom. Fantastic cleverness,
fantastic shortage of wisdom. What goes around comes around.
The boomerang finds its way back.

Grandchildren, grandchildren—objectively, what is so grand?
Little kids are sweet but they turn out to be messed-up humans
like you and me and everybody we like or don't like. Humans
who grow up in the 2040s, 2050s, 2060s, they are going to do
an amazing amount of nasty stuff. And what can they possibly do
on the positive side that we haven't done? All the good human stuff
has been done, we've done it. We cured polio. We produced
Michael Jordan, Kobe Bryant, LeBron James. It's enough!
We went to the fucking moon back in '69 for god's sake.
And on a personal level, we've done a lot of loving
including some great sex (I'm thinking of certain nights
in Savannah) I kid you not. And we've had lunches and dinners
at so many fabulous restaurants—ask me about the pork meatballs
with creamy polenta and the *orecchiette*
at Spiaggia in Chicago, oh my God …
Or think of all the art that has been made—what is the point
of tossing more art on the pile? Art on top of art on top of art
while people are drowning and fighting and starving?
Like, Bosch II, Goya III, Guernica Redux? That's just embarrassing.

You see where I'm coming from. Enough with
"our poor grandchildren"—their big mistake
is showing up way late for the banquet.
Except for my daughter's future kid, to hell with them,
they don't *deserve* a decent life any more than we do.

WHIZDIZZ

Even though you live totally in the whirldazz dazzwhirl
of twenty-first-century simultaneity, if you google
"whirldazz dazzwhirl" you get exactly one hit, which is
a poem by me me me written back in the Nineties
when everything was relatively so simple. Tiny tiny
electronic insects fly everywhere through the billion billion
tubes of our boiling communication hunting for
whirldazz dazzwhirl and finding ONLY ONE appearance
of this (you'll admit) strikingly apt expression
in a poem no one evidently has noticed in the Internet era

whereas there's an infinity of hits for you if you google
data glut or *clickbait* or *twitfame*

and there will be plenty soon if you google
climate refugees or *ecoterror*

so I almost feel that my unique online presence as creator
of the phrase "whirldazz dazzwhirl" turns out to be a quiet oasis,
like a little Meditation Room, and anyone is welcome there
so long as you don't comment, don't forward the link,
let's keep it our secret safe nook strangely unswarmed
by the brilliant fickle hornets of whirldazz dazzwhirl.

SHARK FATE

Curving through the currents undistracted
with tailfin half as long as its body
it watches for those whose luck has been absurd

but the sea is vast and I paddle softly
so it seems quite possible the Thresher will miss me
even quite probable in the mapless blue-black floods

provided I paddle ever softly without splashes
not too close to any school of obvious meatfish
who have not even imagined the strange long tailfin

which suddenly (the books say) whips the water
till life is nothing but panic—oh let me never know
that monstrous slapping and the razor teeth

let me never fathom the unluckiness of South Sudan
or of Yemen or of Syria or of the south side of Chicago
let me swim where misery is a rumor inviting tropes

though my good luck has been absurd and I know it
I say I know it I keep saying I know it
but softly lest that long finned force take an interest

and with absolute concentration move to teach me
how much a minnow with many metaphors matters
and what are the limits of luck in the blue-black floods.

ALMOST DUSK

The time was almost dusk—the sky white silver
over the Walmart parking lot, not only
the lot right in front of Walmart but the larger parking lot
beyond the first lot, all level, almost empty,
there were eight or nine scattered cars
far from where I stood. I stood
out there. I was standing. Under tremendous
white silver sky. Almost dusk.
Far off near Walmart a few old persons moved
very slowly toward bargain prices. There was no story
with a hero. History
and my life and the universe all came to
nothing but this—

even if now, having survived, I am
comfortably seated in the Office for Existential Protest.

AFTER THE MAJOR EVENTS

Footsteps are heard passing through the court without.

The postillions urge the horses to a gallop,
and the carriages are out of sight in a few seconds.

The moon rises, and the ships silently disappear
over the horizon as it mounts higher into the sky.

Hours; days; months; years . . .

Silence prevails, save for the soft hiss of the rain
that falls impartially on both the sleeping armies.

Humans are losingly lost.
A warm summer fog from the Lower Town
covers the Parc and the Place Royale.

Footsteps are heard . . .
Humans are ever lost losers.

The October night thickens and curtains the scene.
Is there an Immanence? If so, it lacks reason.

Rain falls upon lost humans.
The lights are extinguished and the hall is left in darkness.

✳✳✳✳

ANGEL AT WILKES

Brushed by an angel's wing
—the phrase if written in our lifetime is absurd
and god knows I am not religious
but the phrase came to me one night
as I walked across the campus of Wilkes College
in Wilkes-Barre, Pennsylvania, thinking about fidelity—

this was a few months after I married my first wife
and we needed to believe in fidelity—

I saw an earth-moving machine huge and darkly yellow
in the shadows outside a dormitory
and I stood staring at it (because I was needing an epiphany)
until it meant Reality and Realism
and a force or voice was telling me
that marriage would be real in a life of reality
where love would make good sense

different from a life of dizzy bedazzled wishing

and I believed the force or voice was right
and I wanted words for what I felt
staring at the soberly undeluded earth-moving machine
so I said I was *brushed by an angel's wing*

and the marriage was good for about seven years.

The point is not that I was a fool
nor is it that my wife and I were "wrong"
and it's not that the angel idea was absurd—
my feeling is that the angel was real
in one way of being real in life on earth—
though it was an angel of temporary truth.

THEIR FIRST MARRIAGE

It's their first marriage. They seem
happy; she's funny about how she loves
peppermint and hates mayonnaise whereas he feels
the opposite. She likes crossword puzzles
and dislikes chess, he feels the opposite.
He hates Woody Allen, she can't stand Jeremy Irons.
They agree to disagree. They say the differences are
the spice of it all.

They both love Mexican food and trying to speak French
and they agree on lots of important things politically
and they will make a significant effort
at marriage in the Western world in the 21st century.
They could last another six or seven years—or
longer if there's a kid. Obviously

so many things can go wrong but the key problem—
I regret knowing this, I don't want to know it the way I
do feel I know it—the key problem will be
testosterone—or that chemical cocktail that whispers to him
urgently that the world is crammed with shockingly
desirable women whose fascination includes how they are not
his wife. What a world, what a bursting
jungle of a garden of a world! Into which

not to thrust not to pour his glory will seem
eventually a suffocating constriction
no matter how sweet and funny and good she is
over enchiladas and margaritas. But I regret

thinking this and I might be wrong and the guy might be
more grown up than I was and too much European irony can be
debilitating; better maybe to be fiercely
absolute about fidelity like many young lovers—but
in any case one wants to live come what may one wants
to live . . .
        Can it be they already know all this,
just two years into their first marriage?
I almost think I've seen
a sad ironic flicker in her eyes as if she's thought it through.

SARAH SEES TWO RUNNERS

Those two guys running along Sielny Street must be about thirty,
maybe even thirty-five, but they still have that boyish spring
in their stride, that element of gratuitous bounce, though
it's a little more conscious than it was ten years ago,
the boyish spring has a trace of earnest maintenance,
it's something they are pleased to be not losing

as they take Sielny Street at an impressive pace,
fast enough to be impressive without seeming show-offy
and they turn onto Mannlich Avenue without slowing down,
their strong legs bare, rhythmic, hairy in a handsome way,
and it's all admirable, it's fine, it makes sense
in a cardiovascular way, more power to them,
it's fine, there they go with their quality running shoes,
one pair orange and one pair green, navigating
the variations of the old shady sidewalks so fluidly,
thinking how they've really lost nothing
since a decade back, and thinking maybe of
certain female colleagues whom they don't mention to their wives,
and now they're nearly out of sight

though to me still vivid, their strong legs
bare, rhythmic and hairy in a way I have to call
attractive—yet I resent this, I resent
the dumb simplicity of feeling such attraction

while knowing how much more complicated life is
than their loping implies, me here alone on the sidewalk

knowing too much, but of course they have a right
to bounce boyishly as long as they can, in rhythm,
I remember my girlish spring after all
so it's all fine, let them go an extra mile today,
fine, yet I taste something in the mild sunshine
just faintly bitter, reaching in my purse for my keys.

A GENDER THEORY

Women are right:
There must be meaning;
and the meaning will die.

Men are wrong:
They suppose there can be a deathless meaning;
or else that there can be joy without meaning.

Women know the double truth:
There must be meaning;
and the meaning will die.

THE QUILMIAS

In the last decade of his long life my father kept
pictures of several women taped above his desk
including a magazine photo of a shapely young woman
jogging away from the camera in short shorts
and beneath this photo my father had written
They flee from me that sometime did me seek.

Women did find him attractive well into his seventies
and when that power finally faded
the change was deeply puzzling to him
so he needed coping strategies …

Taping up those pictures—he was affirming something
to visitors—or to the ultimate Imagined Friend—
and the understanding smile of the Imagined Friend
was worth more to my father than the sensitivity of anyone
who might consider the pictures "inappropriate" …

When I was in my late fifties I wrote in some notebook
one of the world's billion Older Man Laments—
referring to college women in shorts as
"the long-thighed quilmias"—
I can't find it right now (which may be lucky) but
I liked it and for years I've murmured the phrase
when they strolled away from me in sunlight:
the long-thighed quilmias … Pleasure
of having invented the term—the word glistening for me
between me and the uninterested women—

my old father quoting Wyatt, me inventing a word,
brothers in longing and in coping, seeking
in representation relief from the brunt of longing.

YOUR PALTRY CONQUESTS

I can hardly express how much I don't care about your sex life.
It would be a strain to imagine
anything less interesting. I glimpse a tumbling of limbs in the half-dark
in some depressingly ordinary pragmatic bedroom
and I flinch away from what can do nothing for me but impose
a dreary sordid sense of ubiquitous animal flailing

so remote from the glow of the thrill of the radiance of—
of what I can *almost* in breathless moments remember—
of transcendingness in the one life where this kind of transcendation
can happen and really mean anything

unlike that vulgar thumping and gasping that would be
basically the boring bottom line of any account of
what you did with B and L and H and a dozen others
two dozen whatever all of which is just humiliating I mean
your compulsive exudative mutually delusory *Oh oh oh* business
humiliates *everyone* if I stop and think about it
not that I ever do.

SHADBLOW

What I feel or try to feel is yes okay mutability sure but
for now *seize* and brashly *squeeze*
not to cooperate with the overdetermined washing down
into the muddy culvert obsequious—

if the exaltation is one hour or one astounding minute
or all of April or in a way half of a decade or
three days and nights on the unexpectedly livable west side of town
it will turn out to have been finite

hence haunted by shadow of detritus demolition dispersal
dispossession disjecta dustitude dejection
in the mashed marsh mush of time gone this
is titanically undeniable

but to make it one keen damned thrill of a long hour or minute
as we are symphonious bright marsh marigolds
not yet NOT yet sad trash of shadblow
downdashed to the redundantly mudbashed ditch

and to carry a dream of the minute on beyond the minute
to feel the minute living inside all the downshaded shadblow living
is what I try but it seems to depend on your dream collaboration
which is why abruptly I squeeze your shoulder with awkward admiration.

BEEN THERE

We have been there
in the place where everything in us said welcome
to the other welcome there in that place
where just a thin bar of moonlight or streetlight
glanced into the high room where we were
together in shadows in soft urgencies of thrilled
welcome—it was real it was a real place
high above the ignorant skeptical street
in a sureness we had brilliantly imagined

and to have been there high up secret in that citadel
is to know ever after it is possible
despite whatever hours and years of fumbled
quick goodbyes and buses departing on schedule
and flat cool emails and doormen saying "No longer here."

OUR LOVE PROBLEM

Consummation—total arrival—being utterly there
with the beloved no longer apart—being sheerly
together there in a healing unity of devotedness—

the problem is that we don't feel it is impossible.
We feel it is extremely unlikely
amid the metro noise of two brains being different
(whence our perpetual recycling pivots into humor)
but not impossible—

(because oh darling you do remember what I believe
I remember from nights when dream became truth
you do you must—)

                   and that's enough
to keep us out
              all night on the boulevards
with their dots of distant light

weary but not sleepy
at intersections swerving intuitively left or right
crossing the cobbled plazas
where brisk figures recede into some other life

and pausing on bridges to study the dark river
with its persistent implication which we must refute.

MIDNIGHT, THE STARS AND YOU

Schmaltzy you could say
but in fifty years you'll be gone
and then your judicious preferences will to your ghost seem
less pertinent, less to the point. When Al Bowlly sang in 1934
about seeing the beloved's face in every flower because
she was his Everything the sugar made tolerable the thin
trace of eternal longing—
I'll be remembering for my whole life through
whatever else I do
midnight, the stars and you—

the tooth of it is in how we know it's not true
except in that candlelight where for three minutes it is;

longing as a presence
ever welling up out of the center of the actual
wait let me give
one more example before the next sensitive individual
nudges me away from the podium

yes I know I only have another minute all right
for instance that Rodgers and Hart song "Where or When"
the hour is coming in maybe 2034 when you won't be able to bear it
though you will bear it as we do stuck on the planet of loss
sensing the eternal pattern in our attractions:
some things that happen for the first time seem to be
happening again unbearable lovely or schmaltzy as you say

oh check back with us in fifty years

✳✳✳✳✳

YOU LAMENT

You lament the suffering of others and yet
actually you need the pathos. You need

the exercise—to caringly climb down
from the buzzy elevation
of fretting for neon gratifications
that lead eventually to headaches and insomnia
in the nougat unhealth of nursing
fatly stupid ego.

What saves you is recognizing
pain of others
far and near

—there was that moment in 1975 when my mother slowly
dying in her bed in Westport tried to listen
tried hard focusing her cancer-haunted gaze
when I talked for minutes and minutes about
how Jan (after an affair of two months) "broke my heart"
and suddenly I saw—

NOT NOTHING

To have been there in the years is
(assertion establishing a formation
where erstwhile outspread but tidal ooze)
not nothing.

Must not be just nothing. To have been the one
who said the one thing about a certain book when
no one else was saying that one thing;

to have been among the guests at table
when Gerry burned the oven mitt to a crisp
and Ron presented it—smoking in the tongs—
Mesdames et messieurs—as an entrée . . .
We had our mirth; we had our comradeship

and if I lie awake in some hotel hearing freeway traffic,
feeling infinitesimal—or essentially nonexistent—
this is only a mood and a distortion.

Though Fort Markim in the side yard is gone
(built by our supreme Daddy for Kimbo and me)
and the trapeze behind Charlie Duncan's house is gone

Though Gabriella does not wait to walk with me
into the tall grass

Though I have no evidence that Jan even remembers my name

Though a dozen times at parties or receptions I've done that thing
of locking into intense conversation with one person just met
and revealing in half an hour secrets and regrets and hopes
not brought to light in years of some friendships—
and then realizing there is not a plausible next step—
and then saying goodnight and forgetting...

Though when I do, in the weird ease of electronic life,
suddenly find myself "in touch with" someone
from twenty years ago—or farther—
my ninth-grade English teacher Miss Hastings!—
she was very good—she loved books—
still after four emails there seems to be nothing more to say,
the memory can only be memory...

Though it is egocentrism when an old man feels
we should all listen as he laments the goneness
of his li'l luminous particulars from the Twenties
or Forties or Seventies or whenever—and as egocentrism it is
not only dreary to persons in the first half of life
but also suffocative to persons near his own age (*unless!*—
unless ...)

Though I tried to catch the constant outpouring
in a poem called—what was it called?—the one
about constant loss of the present "all down the chute *whush whush*"
and now even I can't remember—was it "Cascade"?

Though yellow leaves heap up around the house on West 6th
where I lived in a blink of the legendary twentieth century—

still—still what? Though X, still Y—

still I detect *something far more deeply interfused*
when my son smiles at my daughter as if to say
"Dad's getting all too-deep-for-tears again."

WHISK BROOM

In the airport parking lot there was a coat of wet snow
on all the cars that had been there a day longer than mine.
I was sitting in my car checking email with one window half open
when I heard this guy two spaces away talking loud—

to himself. "There is no reason I can't *change* and *grow*."
He was clearing the snow off his car with a small whisk broom,
whisking damp sheets of snow in all directions
with earnest vigorous efficiency—
"I can *escape* the *pathetic repetitions* of my little *habits*
and then Sally will see me with new *respect*."
Snow flicking fast from his car every which way.
"If she thinks I am just another midlife-crisis *turkey*
she has *another—think—coming*!"
Flick, flick, flick—
"And so does Margie and even *Kate*!"

His dark blue Subaru was very free of snow now
but he added a few rhythmic flourishing sweeps
like someone conducting a symphony.
I'm glad the guy didn't notice me,
he might suddenly have felt like such a loser.
But I didn't feel he was a loser, or a turkey—just kind of overwrought.

He got in his car and headed for the exit
and after a minute I followed, to go where I had to go.

ROLF SMEDVIG IN PARTICULAR

A million things ten million good things right in front of me have I missed
but since a sunny morning on Westminster Street on the west side of Providence
I am not totally unaware of Rolf Smedvig!
Because on the radio I heard the Scottish Chamber Orchestra
conducted by Jahja Ling
playing Haydn's Trumpet Concerto in E-flat Major
and the soloist was Rolf Smedvig.
From the perspective of the cognoscenti
I suspect it may be a cliché to "love"
Haydn's bright Trumpet Concerto in E-flat Major
but luckily I am not a cognoscente
so I was free to feel with a fullness
on the sunny west side of Providence
that a marvelous fabulous affirmative thing was achieved
by Rolf Smedvig

                    (who died at sixty-two in 2015)
and for more than six minutes (before my own eventual surrender
to obliviousness) I was filled with gratitude toward Rolf Smedvig—
also toward Jahja Ling and the Scottish Chamber Orchestra
and let's not forget Franz Joseph Haydn—
but especially toward the soloist who represented
the Dauntlessly Proudly Intently Admiring Individual

and *moreover* I became aware that I was grateful for my gratitude toward
in particular Rolf Smedvig.

BUT ALSO

Were there frustrations? Hell yes. There were griping frustrations
and outrageous disappointments and stupid failures
which I will never forget and which would furnish material
for thunderous tragic tales! But also

there was the clink of my spurs as I rode my intelligent black horse
and the arc of a heron suddenly aswoop over the limpid lake
and the pleasure of mentioning European towns and rivers
and buildings and kings and dukes and works of art
and the memory of my father singing "Rocky Raccoon"

and the taste of the caviar Busbacca hid in the goblet
and the pleasure of defying those German boatmen
who claimed we could never climb the brambled hillside
and of later wielding the phrase "German boatmen" superciliously
and the comedy of Busbacca trying to outdrink Hans
and then shouting in his sleep about demons
who schemed to drown him and steal his caviar
though he was ready enough to ride forth in the morning

and there was the gentle curve of the road that led us to Zurich
where we cleaned our clothes, and the feel of clean linen next day
and the possibility I believed I saw
in the eyes of Angelica as she stood in the doorway
and watched us ride out of the straw-sprinkled inn-yard

and we rode to Solothurn and from there to Lausanne,
from Lausanne to Geneva, from Geneva to Lyons,
and much of the way we were singing like thrushes, like larks,
like larks who know how to enjoy good claret.

MY OTHER APARTMENT

It's on a street between two more visible streets
so you have to recognize a certain repair shop on the corner
I've walked right past it and not realized till years later

The building is calmly old in a gentle reliable way
and the stairs creak in a way that confirms their existence
Not often have I been there but I maintain the place

for the knowing that it is there, a knowing which
once in a while becomes a compelling knowledge
so that I wend my way carefully along shady sidewalks

past the more obvious intersections and stroll closer
and pause and think and move and eventually reach
my other apartment—though only after a few odd

deflections and distractions in a cloudy world seeming
arranged to impede my arrival at the old calm door—
eventually there I am on the gray perceptible stairs

and I have a key for the sturdy gray door
and I see that certain items are waiting for me
in the right places, meaningfully located;

there is a back room, a room not obvious but quietly
reachable, where certain books are placed in rows
on a table, or two tables, alongside certain notebooks ...

What is in the notebooks? I almost remember:
they are filled with the understandings that never quite
took shape except there; if they are slightly eccentric,

quietly peculiar, that will be their secret glory;
again and again I cross the threshold into the back room
to see the books and notebooks waiting in rows—

there they are—there they are—with a rightness
which fills the air of the apartment giving validation
to me and to the dish of black olives on the Formica table

and to the Kandinsky prints on the walls
and to the Haydn symphony on the radio softly
and so it makes sense if a woman—if a woman—
has there not been a woman perhaps with dark brown skin
a woman gentle and wise who has visited me there
and have we not talked about James Baldwin

and loved some of his paragraphs together? And
was she not glad to be with me and nowhere else,
glad to encourage some previously unguessed fulfillment
in my other apartment?

PLOT TWIST

It turns out that our boy's mother is not dead after all.
This is in Chapter 32. Earlier there were extremely subtle hints
but a reader can be forgiven for not picking them up.
So Chapter 32 comes as quite a stunner. We discover
that an elaborate chain of errors—misunderstandings,
but also lies—an extraordinary conjunction of deceptions
and eerie coincidences—all this believable though just barely—
this maddening conspiracy of bad faith and bad luck—
has hidden the fact that our boy's mother is alive!

What at last emerges is that his old friend's Scottish aunt,
that is, the Scottish uncle's supposed sister, in Fife,
is actually the woman who vanished in the museum in Chapter 9.
In other words she is the mother of our boy. Why
did she keep her survival secret for all these years?
It's complicated. She felt she had no choice.
She was the victim of an astounding scheme—
because of her beauty and her kindness and because of
what somebody knew she knew about what happened
that day in Vancouver in Chapter 6—she

with her light brown hair and her hazel eyes,
her eyes so quick and alert, the way she combined
alertness with love—and everything—it turns out
she is not dead! This is in Chapter 32. It's complicated
and it's a long time coming but you have to keep reading,
no matter what, keep going till the end.

NO VACATION FOR MAIGRET

Fifty years ago my mother's hands held this detective novel.
She knew the world included secret passions, vile schemes, threats.
Who killed Lili Godreau? The question should not be left unanswered!

From Poitiers come two young detectives, Piéchard and Boivert,
they are not stupid but they lack intuition.
When a second murder happens they have no clue.
But Inspector Maigret is staring into certain memories.

Who was the frightened girl on the stairs?
Fourteen years old, with reddish hair, black stockings,
and a small purse covered with colored beads—who was she?
She was Lucile Duffieux
and now she has been murdered—because she knew too much
about Lili Godreau? My mother's hands hold these pages
fifty years ago … Maigret's eyes take in the details,
nothing is too small to notice when a girl has met such a fate—

in the yard at the Duffieux house there is a pallid sandy garden
with five tomato plants, leeks, lettuce, cabbages,
and in one corner a rabbit hutch; Maigret gives the rabbits
a few cabbage leaves because a little kindness is better than
despair; he is thinking and my mother watches him thinking
fifty years ago. Lucile Duffieux, that decent frightened girl is dead
and so is Lili Godreau—the world allows such losses!
Someone must answer back, someone must respond
to arrogant ruthless cruelty! A strong enough woman can answer back

but until she's ready there's the gruff Inspector
who has canceled his vacation to study the clues—
and Maigret has an idea.

MEANING

Days and the days. They clank like freight cars
manufactured only to clank and not deliver the goods
to sweet children over the mountain. The engineer must come!
Let him climb up to the high swaying cab
and select shiny black coals of history
at last made handy: so events will burn into story.
So not be just the littered helpless yards of Camden.
The air is gray the walls are gray the floor is gray and the days clank

so the M thing is wanted:
lest all be the sewer gush.
Lest all be unscrew your jammed ignition rotor and screw in a new one
made to specs with a view to maximum mileage; won't be all
mere fludge of bits tattered across the cinders
alongside the drim-drimming tracks.
What is it can keep you—keep you
unbowed passing the poor low yards
unbowed even if not unfazed as the clank train passes
the thousand small poor yards of Camden
so they don't become the center or base or junked core
and one smear-nosed child way down there alone
chucking half a brick at a brown beer bottle
doesn't helplessly sum up all we ever are allowed to be.
More than a station our destination: the M thing . . .

What is deeper than the days something must be what is?
Don't say God you know that's only codeine stand up straight
match up your socks in pairs and shut the dresser drawer
something must—

I see me walking south on 8th Street with five books in a bag
walking west through Watertown with three books in a bag
walking down Angell Street forty-some years ago with six bagged books
possibly containing that M thing. Never did read
most of those books but someth—something must have stayed—
from Dostoevsky in my 1970 head it may be:
Let us remember Ilusha's face and his clothes and his poor little boots,
Alyosha said. And his coffin, and his unhappy father,
and how boldly Ilusha stood up for him alone against the whole school.
…Something
not blotted in all the drimming fludge.
Without this
so much concern weirdly unsolid all glog in the gush
down sewer gone; clank of the freight cars along practick track

but the other—that other calls. M thing.